UPTOWN

❖

*Portait of a
Chicago Neighborhood
in the Mid-1970s*

Bob Rehak

CHICAGO'S BOOKS PRESS

CONTENTS

Introduction	5
Images	16
Tools and Techniques	270
Acknowledgements	272

Copyright © 2013 Rehak Creative Services, Inc.
All rights reserved.

First printing, 2013.

Published in the United States of America in 2013
by Chicago's Books Press,
an imprint of Chicago's Neighborhoods, Inc.

All photographs and text by Robert Rehak.

Designed by Mike Meyers of Rehak Creative Services.

Printed in Canada by Friesens Corporation.

For further information about this book email brehak@rehak.com
or nsamors@comcast.net or visit bobrehak.com.

ISBN: 978-0-9852733-3-0 (hard cover)
ISBN: 978-0-9852733-4-7 (soft cover)

Front cover - *Praying man on the corner of Wilson and Broadway. When asked if he would mind being photographed, he dropped to his knees and said, "My name is Jehovah." See more details of this shot in the introduction and on page 246.*

Lurker — *While photographing someone else, I turned and found this man staring blankly at me with a drug pipe in his left hand. Drugs had become such a problem in America during the 1960s that President Nixon declared a War on Drugs in 1971. Uptown's many abandoned and burned out buildings were a magnet for drug dealers and users in the mid-1970s. Many also used drugs openly on the streets.*

Wilson Looking East From 'L' — *During the mid-1970s. I took several shots from this position, but this was the only one taken with a 300mm telephoto. I bought the lens in New York on 34th Street. I was almost mugged for it when I left the store. Ironically, during four years of photographing in Uptown, I was never threatened once. Note: of the 40+ cars in this shot, only one is a compact. Can you spot it?*

INTRODUCTION

IN 1972, WHILE STILL IN GRADUATE SCHOOL, I began working in downtown Chicago. Every day, I rode the elevated train (the 'L') between the Far North Side where I lived and my office. On the way, I passed through a neighborhood called Uptown.

Uptown at the time fascinated and frightened me. From the 'L', I caught glimpses of:
- *Streets littered with garbage*
- *Broken pavement and sidewalks*
- *A flop house advertising rooms for 75 cents per night*
- *Winos passed out on sidewalks or drinking on doorsteps*
- *Amputees on crutches dressed in tattered clothes*
- *Stolen, stripped and abandoned cars*
- *Crumbling, boarded-up, burned-out buildings covered with gang graffiti*
- *Men, women and children lined up outside day labor agencies*
- *Taverns, resale shops and pawn shops stretching as far as I could see*

Poor Whites, Blacks, Asians, Hispanics, Native Americans, Indians, Europeans, the young, the old, the drunk, the sober, the sane and barely functional were all crowded together in one of Chicago's most densely populated neighborhoods.

Just blocks away, but a world away, I could also see the high-rise apartment buildings of Chicago's elite. Their buildings formed a wall along Lake Shore Drive. They were also technically part of Uptown.

I felt drawn to Uptown, yet frightened by it. I could not get the images out of my mind and constantly wondered, "How did Uptown become what it is?"

During this period, I studied the work of great documentary photographers. They included Mathew Brady, Jacob Riis, Roy Stryker, Dorothea Lange, W. Eugene Smith, Walker Evans, Margaret Bourke-White, Bruce Davidson, Bob Edelman, Diane Arbus, and – in a class by himself – Arthur Fellig, a.k.a. Weegee. Someone once asked Weegee for the secret of his success. He replied, "F8 and be there."

When I read this, I realized that I had to overcome my fear of Uptown if I was going to photograph there. The fear took two forms: fear for my safety and fear of asking strangers, many of them disabled and disfigured, if I could photograph them.

INTRODUCTION – *continued*

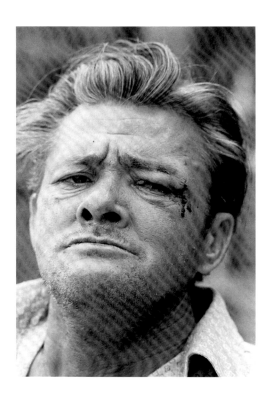

It took a year to work up the courage, but by late 1973, I did it. One Saturday, I grabbed my Nikon F2, got on the 'L', and got off at Wilson Avenue. On the street, I saw a man with a fedora and tattered jacket chomping on the end of a stubby cigar (see cover and pages 78, 246). He was pacing nervously and muttering to himself in front of a Greek restaurant on the corner of Broadway and Wilson. With my heart pounding, I walked right up to him and said, "Can I take your picture?"

I'll never forget what happened next. He flashed me a big smile and said, "Sure!" Then as I put my camera up to my eye, he suddenly dropped to his knees and assumed a praying posture. I quickly dropped to my knee and focused as he shouted, "My name is Jehovah." Click. I had captured my first shot in Chicago's Uptown.

Later that night, while developing the film, I got another surprise. The man was missing parts of two fingers. Everything had happened so quickly that I hadn't even noticed it while taking the shot.

I met many equally interesting people that day. Much to my surprise and delight, no one beat me over the head or tried to steal my camera. In fact, I realized that all my fears had been unjustified. The people were remarkably open and welcoming. They felt flattered that someone was paying attention to them and listening to their concerns.

Thus began my four-year love affair with photographing the people of Uptown. I went there on weekends and holidays to capture the rich diversity of street life. My objective was to capture the personality of the neighborhood by photographing the people who comprised it. Each outing was a visual treasure hunt. From late 1973 to early 1977, I shot approximately 5,000 images in Uptown. Most focused on people; a few focused on objects, businesses and architecture in one of America's greatest melting pots.

How Did Uptown Become Uptown?

Several factors conspired to make Uptown what it had become by the mid-1970s. They included:

- *The neighborhood's origin as an entertainment center*
- *The style of architecture that became popular there in the 1920s*
- *The growth of suburbia after World War II that lured away many middle-class families*

- *Redevelopment of other parts of Chicago that dislocated the city's poor and pushed them toward Uptown*
- *The de-institutionalization of mental patients*
- *The OPEC oil embargo of 1973 that drove unemployment to 9.8% and inflation to 12.34%*
- *Political activists trying to preserve low-income housing for the poor by stalemating developers trying to construct new buildings.*

The result was a perfect storm of humanity, economics, and legislation that made Uptown "ground zero" for poverty.

Uptown Had a Glorious Past
When the Northwestern Elevated Railroad established service to Wilson Avenue in 1900, a housing boom followed.

High land values in the 1920s encouraged construction of luxurious apartments. Uptown's population doubled. Newspapers back then speculated that Uptown might grow to eclipse Chicago's downtown.

At one time, the business barons of Chicago had their summer homes here. Charlie Chaplin and Gloria Swanson, film stars from the silent era, produced movies at the Essanay Studios on Argyle Street. The Riviera Theater (1917), Aragon Ballroom (1926), and Uptown Theatre (1926) turned Uptown into Chicago's premier entertainment district. These ornate theaters ushered in a Gilded Age for Uptown. The Uptown Theater seated 4,320 people! It was the third largest in America when it opened in terms of seating capacity and the largest in square footage; it was billed as "An Acre of Seats in a Magic City."

During this era, bars, dance halls and nightclubs proliferated throughout Uptown as part of the area's focus on entertainment. They catered to young singles, flocking to the area for its nightlife.

Unique Architectural Style
The influx of young professionals encouraged construction of a new type of residence during this period, known as apartment hotels. They offered a cosmopolitan lifestyle, free of household drudgery and long commutes. The Lawrence Apartment Hotel in Uptown advertised itself as a "fine club," with luxurious lobbies and a dazzling array of

INTRODUCTION – *continued*

modern services including an indoor driving range, gymnasium, pool and rooftop solarium.

Social life was paramount, so apartments were small. Most had only a single room. They came fully furnished with Murphy beds that folded up into walls. Rents included maid service. Meals were taken in the hotels' lavish dining rooms and cafés. Who wanted to spend time cleaning a large apartment and cooking? The action and excitement were in Uptown's theaters and clubs.

Developers built more than 70 apartment hotels similar to the Lawrence in Uptown. The Lawrence leased its 400 one-room apartments before the building was completed – seven months before the stock market crashed in 1929.

These giant apartment hotels later came to be known as SROs (for single resident occupancy). SRO tenants typically shared bathrooms and/or kitchens, but some SRO rooms included kitchenettes, bathrooms, or half-baths. Ironically, almost half a century after they were built, these facilities attracted an entirely different type of resident for entirely different reasons.

Uptown's population soared during the Depression. The large stock of housing attracted migrants and, later, war workers, seeking jobs in Chicago. However, during the 1930s, Uptown also developed a reputation for boisterous taverns and rowdy entertainment. Respectable middle-class families began their exodus to the suburbs.

The Lure of Suburbs After World War II
G.I.s returning from World War II accelerated this trend. The G.I. bill encouraged the rapid growth of suburbia after 1945 by providing help for more than 3.5 million low-interest home mortgages. At the program's peak, in 1947, approximately 40 percent of all housing starts in the nation were funded by guarantees in the bill. By 1955, 4.3 million home loans had been granted under the G.I. bill.

In the 1950s, Uptown was like an aging starlet living off the fading glory of its yellowing press clippings. SROs began catering to low-income migrants from the South and Appalachia with rents as low as three dollars per day. They filled the vacuum left by the middle class.

Redevelopment of Chicago's Near North During the 1960s

During the 1960s, as suburbs stretched ever further north and west, commuting times became intolerable. People began moving back into the city. The first wave of new urban pioneers settled north of Chicago's downtown – in Old Town and Lincoln Park.

From this base, redevelopment marched relentlessly north during the 1960s and early 1970s. Young professionals bought brownstones. They put in new windows, electricity, plumbing, and hardwood floors. After re-plastering and painting, they flipped properties quickly for handsome profits. I had one friend at Leo Burnett who became a millionaire before he was 30 by renovating brownstones during this era.

Poor Pushed North Toward Uptown

Higher rents for newly renovated properties pushed the poor even further north … to Uptown. The same phenomenon happened when the University of Illinois Chicago Circle Campus was built on the west side; many of the displaced moved to Uptown.

The Puerto Ricans who had settled in Old Town in the 1950s were among the first to migrate north. Waves of Asians, Hispanics, Native Americans, and African-Americans followed them; so did poor Whites. Uptown also became a port of entry for migrants from the South and Appalachia looking for work.

By the late 1960s, Uptown was already known as "Hillbilly Heaven" because of all the poor southern whites who lived there. According to *Uptown: Poor Whites in Chicago*, Todd Gitlin and Nanci Hollander's 1971 sociological study, as many as half of Uptown's estimated 50,000 residents were southern born. There were so many that, at one point, they proposed a plan to redevelop the Wilson train yards as "Hank Williams Village," for the great country singer.

Deinstitutionalization

About this time, Illinois (and many other states) began deinstitutionalizing the patients of mental hospitals; it was a national trend started during the Kennedy administration. Uptown absorbed an estimated 7,000 of them. Thanks to the development of new drugs, these people were marginally functional. Halfway homes in Uptown

INTRODUCTION – *continued*

received approximately 40% of all those released into Chicago, despite the fact that Uptown comprised only 1% of Chicago's landmass.

By the early 1970s, Uptown had the second highest population density in Chicago and high unemployment. It had become skid row. Just when you thought things couldn't get any worse, they did.

OPEC Embargo Triggers High Unemployment and Inflation

The OPEC oil embargo in October, 1973, quadrupled oil prices from $3 to $12 per barrel within months. Inflation jumped from 3.65% before the embargo to 12.64% in 1974. This triggered a massive, nationwide recession that persisted for a decade.

Unemployment went from 3.7% at the start of the decade to 8.7% by 1975 and reached a high of 9.7% in 1982, slightly higher than the 9.6% reached in 2010 during America's most recent "Great Recession."

After the embargo, few could afford to drive the large, gas-guzzling cars that Detroit had been producing. Domestic auto sales plummeted; compact foreign cars gained a toehold in America.

A Shakespearean Tragedy in the Making

Other social forces also transformed Uptown during the early 1970s:
- *In the 1960s, activist groups, such as the Students for a Democratic Society (SDS) and Black Panthers began organizing neighborhood protests against slumlords. To preserve low income housing for Uptown's poor, other activist groups joined in. They slowed the pace of redevelopment and, in many cases, stalemated it.*
- *Some landlords used extreme tactics, such as arson, to evict tenants so that they could redevelop their properties. Physical neglect, vandalism, and arson resulted in as many as 400 fires in a single year. According to a Chicago fireman who worked in Uptown for many years, Engine Company 83 (the Uptown Station) was the busiest in America during the decade of the 1970s and early 1980s.*
- *From 1972 through 1974, the Watergate Scandal distracted America's attention from pressing social problems.*
- *The Vietnam War was still in full swing, diverting as much as 9.5% of America's gross domestic product, according to Congressional reports.*
- *A drug culture was taking root in America.*

By the time I stepped off the 'L' in 1973, Uptown had reached rock bottom; it had become ground zero for poverty and urban decay. The pictures on the following pages were taken primarily during 1974, 1975 and 1976, as I walked virtually every street in the neighborhood.

Some of these images may not fall within the technical boundaries of Uptown today. Those boundaries have changed over time – areas such as Edgewater, Buena Park and Sheridan Park "seceded" from Uptown to distance themselves from its reputation.

Life Lessons Learned Early

It would be easy to look at the people on these pages and blame their poverty on bad choices or slothfulness. It would also be wrong.

On my first day in Uptown, I was skeptical about how hard working the people there were. Certainly, some had given up and were content to live off welfare.

But I also met a 13-year-old girl who screwed caps on shampoo bottles for 12 hours per day. She worked for one of Uptown's many day-labor agencies and brought home about $10 per day to help feed herself and her family. Lazy? I think not.

I met a man who came to Chicago from Arkansas in 1974 shortly after the OPEC oil embargo to look for work. He had just $9 in his pocket and no friends in the city. He spent his first night at the Wilson Club Men's Hotel, a notorious flophouse. The next day, he waited at a day-labor agency until 3 p.m. before they assigned him a backbreaking job that no one else would take – doing demolition work. He earned enough to buy a $2 steak at a nearby café that night and a $3 per night room at a slightly better hotel. Lazy? I think not.

I heard many stories from people I trusted about friends who worked 12-hour shifts for day-labor agencies, but did not get paid. The first time I heard this, I was skeptical. The twentieth time I heard it, I was furious. One employer reportedly said, "Why should I pay him? He'll just drink it up anyway?"

It's one thing to try to understand Uptown by studying statistics – another to smell it and feel it. Learning the stories of these people may make you much more compassionate and much less judgmental.

Wild-Hair Day – *Blame it on the Windy City. It didn't seem to embarrass her or diminish her enthusiasm for life. Like most of the kids I met in Uptown, she was filled with boundless energy and seemed undaunted by the poverty around her.*

INTRODUCTION – *continued*

Role Models and The Wheel of Life

As I scanned hundreds of negatives for this book and reread my notes from 40 years ago, I got to know these people all over again. With time and distance, I could see several things more clearly.

I was struck by the innocence, enthusiasm and boundless energy of the children. As one told me recently, "We could turn anything into a game." When I first met him, he was ten years old and playing with friends on a broken couch thrown from the fourth floor of a walk-up.

No kid "chose" to grow up in Uptown, but those who survived it were somewhat richer and stronger for the experience. Others were emotionally scarred for life. In many poor families, relationships are often neglected because survival comes first; parents leave kids unattended while they work long hours. Those children often learn from role models they see around themselves on the streets.

By the time kids reached their early teens, many started to gravitate toward gangs like the Latin Kings, Latin Eagles, Harrison Gents, Gaylords, Unknowns, and Thorndale Jagoffs. Why did kids join these gangs? Some were drawn to the parties, girls and drugs. Some were looking for a chance to make money. And some joined for self-protection. But I think most were looking for a "family." They wanted friends, acceptance, attention and respect. The gangs filled those needs.

Most of the adults I met in the 20- to 40-year-old age range were busy trying to make rent payments and put food on the table. Those who had families often *needed* dual incomes to *survive*. This frequently left kids home alone for long stretches without supervision. Loneliness often helped push them toward gangs.

In Uptown, everyone struggled to survive and to achieve some semblance of normalcy in their lives while surrounded by winos, addicts, decay, violence, bar fights and halfway homes.

Many have contacted me through my photoblog to say that – despite the adversity – Uptown was the most memorable experience in their lives. Uptown contained characters more incredible than those found in any circus sideshow. Despite their poverty or perhaps because of it, I found them to be some of the most welcoming people I have ever met.

Uptown is very different today; it's much improved. That's a tribute to hard-working people with vision who never gave up on Uptown. But that's a story for another book. For now, strap yourself into the way-back machine.

UPTOWN

*Portrait of a
Chicago Neighborhood
in the Mid-1970s*

The Big Leagues – *I saw a group of jovial kids coming toward me with a baseball bat and asked if I could take a picture. The kid with the bat immediately struck a Mark McGwire pose (years before Mark McGwire became a phenomenon). The other kids crowded around just so they could be in the shot, too. I often look at this shot and wonder whether their innocent enthusiasm survived the neighborhood.*

Recycled – *Collecting soda bottles from trash cans used to be a way for kids to make money. They would take bottles they found to grocery stores and collect a nickel deposit. Back in the 1970s, you could still buy a candy bar for that nickel. Unfortunately, it wasn't enough to buy shoes.*

Uptown Jungle Gym – *Kids in suburban neighborhoods had playgrounds with jungle gyms. At Winthrop and Ainslie, there were no playgrounds, so these kids competed in tree climbing. The limb that the boy on the left is standing on fell after I snapped this shot. Fortunately, he wasn't hurt. Uptown kids were tough.*

Staying Warm – *Memorial Day of 1976 must have been a cold day in Chicago's Uptown. I found this man trying to stay warm by a barrel with a fire.*

Drunk Passed Out – *Photographing on Sunday mornings during the 1970s in Uptown was always interesting. On this day, I found a drunk passed out on the hood of a car outside one of the neighborhood's many bars. Kids were playing nearby. No one seemed to pay much attention to this man. I remember being surprised that no one had stolen the rest of his drink.*

Pages 22-23
Uptown Theater and Green Mill Lounge – *Just north of Lawrence on Broadway lie two Uptown landmarks. The Uptown is a spectacular Balaban and Katz theater from Chicago's Gilded Age and larger than Radio City Music Hall. When I took this picture in 1976, "Killer Force" starring O.J. Simpson was playing. The Green Mill Lounge hosted jazz groups and poets. It opened for business in 1907 as Pop Morse's Roadhouse. The Book Box, now also operating under a different name, has been owned by the same family for 47 years.*

Chelsea Hotel – Built in 1923 on Wilson near Sheridan, the Chelsea was one of Uptown's original apartment hotels. Like many such establishments, it fell into disrepair after World War II. In 1967, real-estate developer Leonard Richman converted it into a retirement hotel for seniors. It stood out in Uptown; it was well maintained and had a uniformed doorman.

Walkie-Talkie Man – At Wilson and Sheridan, down the block from the Sheridan Plaza Hotel, the man sitting on a parked car was talking to someone with his walkie-talkie. Cell phones had not been invented yet. The sidewalk badly needed repair – like most of Chicago's Uptown neighborhood in the mid-1970s.

Man in Need at Salvation Army – *The people of Uptown had a deep respect for the Salvation Army. Its mission was and is, "To meet human needs in God's name without discrimination." In December, 1974, when I took this shot, the Salvation Army operated a kitchen on Wilson Avenue. This man hoped to get some food, but was too proud to ask for help. He hadn't eaten in several days.*

Engine 83 – *I took this shot at the corner of Wilson and Broadway on April 26, 1975. Engine 83 came around the corner first with sirens blaring. Engine 83 was the busiest fire company in the U.S. during the 1970s and early 1980s, according to a firefighter who worked at the Uptown Fire Station on Wilson during that era.*

Cop Helping Blind Man – *Several people walked past this blind man attempting to cross the very busy intersection of Broadway and Wilson. Then this cop spotted him and escorted him across the street. I've always marveled at how a blind man could navigate around the potholes, litter and broken sidewalks in Uptown during this era.*

Popsicles – *What more could kids want on a hot summer day? Like so many of the kids in Uptown, they seemed happy despite the poverty. They had not yet been ground down by life. "We did not know we were in poverty because we saw our mothers get up and go to work everyday," the one on the right wrote me 39 years later. "We really did not want for much growing up." All three live in Chicago suburbs today.*

Kung Fu Kid – *In the mid-1970s, kung fu movies were the rage on television. Kids constantly struck martial arts poses. This one took it to a new level to impress his young girlfriend.*

Winthrop Near Ainslie – *In 1975, the center of Latin King activity in Uptown was on this corner. You can see their graffiti scrawled on several of the buildings here. The bleakness of this shot – police cruiser, dented cars, gang graffiti, boarded up windows, man with a cane, and a beer truck – symbolizes much of Uptown in the mid-1970s.*

Wilson and Broadway – *This shot was taken from under the 'L' on a cold day in December, 1975. Then, it seemed like there was a plywood news stand near every 'L' stop. The Internet, smartphones and wireless networks would not become practical realities for another 25 years. People consumed news on paper and newspapers cost just 15 cents.*

It's the Thought that Counts – *During December of 1974, the Salvation Army operated a soup kitchen on Wilson Avenue just east of Broadway. I took this shot of their Santa greeting clients. Hollywood he wasn't. But when you're hungry, you tend to overlook little details. I'm sure everyone appreciated the effort.*

Under the 'L' – *Historically, businesses benefit from proximity to mass transit. In 1975, businesses bustled underneath these tracks. The view is from the west side of Broadway, looking south toward Wilson. In the background, you can see Walgreens and the Bissets Department store that used to be on the corner of Wilson and Broadway. According to the CTA, between 5,000 and 6,000 riders per day board the 'L' at the Wilson Station.*

Prize Fighter – The man in the white suit told me that he was a professional prize fighter who fought under the name "Spider Webb." He even gave me his manager's name and phone number … just in case I knew of someone who wanted to fight him. I was photographing him when one of his fans came out of a bar.

Formal – Uptown in the 1920s was home to Chicago's rich and famous. Despite the neighborhood's decline, some of the original residents stayed on. During the 1960s, most American women fell out of love with the hat. But in 1974, when I took this shot, some older people still clung to the tradition, especially when they went to church.

Trixie — *I grabbed this shot at 1000 West Argyle in February of 1976. All dogs love cheese. This man joked that Trixie loved Brie. Trixie looked like she really did. The man had fought in North Africa with the French Foreign Legion before settling in Chicago.*

The White Dress – *This young girl was playing on her apartment's front steps. Despite temperatures in the twenties, she had no jacket. She shivered as I took her photo. Many families in Uptown could not afford clothes or shoes for their children. Still, they managed somehow.*

Outward Appearances – *Acne this severe would make most people reluctant to have their photo taken. But this man didn't mind. Despite his fearsome appearance, he seemed like a gentleman and we had a nice conversation.*

Uptown Playground – *During the mid-1970s, it seemed alleys and vacant lots were the closest thing Uptown had to playgrounds. Of course, there were a few neighborhood schools and Lincoln Park, but kids felt safer playing closer to home. Navigating streets filled with drunks and gangs could be far more dangerous than playing in a back alley.*

Best Friends — *This shot epitomized Uptown in the mid-1970s — one man smoking a corn cob pipe while hugging his hydrocephalic buddy outside a halfway house. Both were gentle souls. The man on the left looked after the man on the right.*

"No Pitty" (sic) – *This shot always seemed like an omen. An innocent boy walking his dog in front of a mural that says, "We have no pitty in Latin King City." The Latin Kings may have ruled the streets of Uptown in the 1970s, but they had not yet mastered spelling. Every time I look at this shot, I wonder if this boy got swept up in gang violence as he grew older.*

Stripped – *During the night, thieves stripped this vehicle. They took its hubcaps, wheels, mirrors, battery and dignity. Mercifully, they also stole the wipers so police couldn't leave a ticket on the windshield for an expired parking meter. I have a friend who once parked his car in Uptown during this era. When he returned, thieves were stealing his front wheels. He confronted them. "What the @#$% are you guys doing?" he shouted. They replied, "No problem. You take the back wheels." Incredibly, they thought he was another thief and were offering to share the spoils. Scenes like this were common in Uptown during this era.*

Father and Adopted Daughter – *This girl's mother came to Chicago from West Virginia looking for work. She and the girl were living on the streets when the man took them into his home, married the mother and adopted the daughter. Visceral reactions to this image among both black and white Americans tell you how deeply ingrained racism remains in American culture.*

Pocketknife – *A boy's first pocketknife is a right of passage. This young man was trying to imitate older Uptown gang members. Or was he trying to imitate Frank Sinatra with that hat?*

Pages 52-53
Latin Eagles – *One day while photographing this mural, I found myself surrounded by gang members. I offered to take their picture and later gave each of them prints. This simple act of kindness helped guarantee me safe passage on the streets. I spent four years photographing there and never felt threatened or hassled. The flag is Puerto Rican and Hipolito Vega is most likely the mural's painter.*

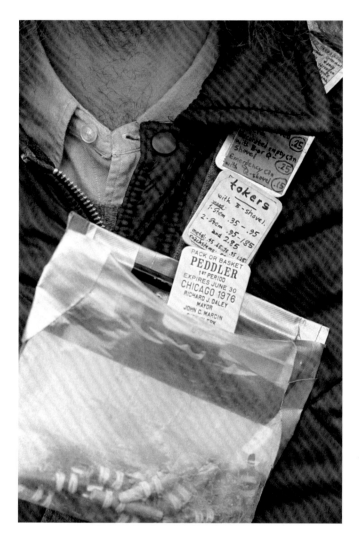

Peddling Drug Paraphernalia – *I thought this young man would run when he saw me raising my camera to take a picture. Instead he smiled and proudly displayed a City of Chicago license for street peddlers. After I took about two dozen shots of him, he even signed my model release form.*

Lotta Love – *The poverty in Uptown often kept parents working around the clock, but sometimes it also forged extremely close family ties. If it weren't for the fact that this man had his child wrapped around his shoulders, I would swear the child had him wrapped around his little finger.*

The Lone Teardrop – *I took this on a wintry Thanksgiving morning. It was so cold, the heat from my body fogged the ground glass of my Rollei SL66. Only after developing the image and printing it did I see the tear in the woman's eye. She was on her way to a shelter, where hopefully she found some Thanksgiving food. It was never clear to me whether the tear was caused by the cold or her situation.*

Sex or Love – *Back in 1976, 4138 North Sheridan was the international headquarters of Mona Girl Cosmetics, which also sold 8-track tapes, cigars, lottery tickets, and sex or love. The store was a hangout for Uptown's under-10 crowd as you can see by the bikes in the doorway.*

Rug Merchant – *Street vendors would pop up on corners throughout Uptown during the mid-1970s. This man was a rug merchant who proudly displayed his goods to all passing by. I know of at least one person who purchased one to cover a hole in a wall. The merchant was a Palestinian from Jerusalem who spoke little English. He worked Broadway for approximately 30 years. A local pizza shop held a memorial for him when he died.*

Old Japanese Man – *Uptown in the 1970s was a true melting pot; people from many different cultures were packed together here. Many Asians populated the northern parts of the neighborhood. There, I photographed this man on a cold January day in 1975. His eyes were filled with kindness, wisdom and understanding.*

The Third Eye — *I found this woman standing on the street in front of a halfway house. When she talked, she seemed normal enough. I was just taken aback by the jewel pasted to her forehead and surrounded by Pentel marks. She seemed oblivious to it until I asked her what it was. She told me, "The third eye!" I might have thought she was a mystic had it not been for the children's plastic keys around her neck.*

Pop-Top Gun Fun – *This kid crafted a rubber-band gun out of a scrap of wood, a nail, a clothes pin and a giant rubber band. It shot pop tops hard enough to break windows or skin. The photo was taken near Winthrop and Ainslie.*

Two Hats – *This man was a musician from Ireland. He told me he lived on the streets and slept on a bus bench. He had to wear all his clothes to avoid having them stolen. It was common for such people to be attacked, beaten and robbed while they slept.*

Deliverance – In 1972, a movie called "Deliverance" starring John Voight topped box offices around the country. The theme song of this hit movie about life in Appalachia was "Dueling Banjos." Two pickers strummed at ever faster rates until they reached speeds that were seemingly impossible for humans. On Wilson Avenue in the summer of 1974, I found these two men strumming the same tune but with a banjo and a guitar. They were almost as good as the pickers in the movie. During the 1970s, Uptown was often called "Hillbilly Heaven" because of all the people who migrated here from Appalachia. The Wooden Nickel bar in the background catered to the country crowd. It frequently booked performers like these.

Home Sweet Home – *I found this man walking back to his apartment on crutches, trying to carry a bag of groceries from a store more than a mile away. I asked him why. He had been "jack-rolled by four Indians." They had broken his ankle, then taken his wallet, money, paycheck, keys and car. He had come to Chicago from Kentucky for a job as a machine operator. But with no car, he lost his job. Then his wife left him. He tried to get on welfare, but visiting all the required offices was difficult on crutches. There were grocery stores closer to his apartment, but none would give him credit till he got back on his feet. I helped him carry the groceries back to his apartment where he allowed me to take several shots.*

Playing Hooky – *I photographed this ninth grader on the first day of school in the fall of 1974. He told me he was playing hooky because he wanted to get into a private school. He also talked about how dope dealers would hunt you down if you turned them in. He wanted to be a policeman because "they make good money." But in the next breath he said, "I wouldn't turn my friends in even if they were dealing because you can't turn on your friends."*

Best Friends – *The boy on the right moved with his family to Uptown from Kentucky. When I asked these two if I could take their picture, they threw their arms around each others' shoulders and announced that they were "best friends." Their happiness was short lived. His oldest brother reportedly became one of John Wayne Gacy's first victims shortly after I took this photo. Gacy found many of his victims in Uptown.*

Pages 70-71
Resale Sale – *Uptown in the mid-1970s was filled with resale shops. They often displayed merchandise on sidewalks and tried to look as "no frills" as possible to attract the attention of Uptown's budget conscious shoppers. However, this shop set a new standard. In keeping with the bare bones decor, the owner ripped the "for" off of a "for sale" sign. Even the lady's dog is cringing when it walked by this shop.*

The Thousand Yard Stare — *I don't know much about this man. I took only one shot of him, then he walked off without saying a word. The term "Thousand Yard Stare" was coined during World War II to describe the unfocused gaze of battle-weary soldiers. When I was photographing in Uptown, thousands of vets were returning from Vietnam with post-traumatic stress disorder. Perhaps he was one of them.*

Uptown Fashion Plates – *This man was a gang leader who went by the street name of Pinhead. When I asked if I could photograph him, his girlfriend jumped in the shot and struck a pose reminiscent of a fashion model. People in Uptown during this era often felt ignored by the world; the mere presence of a photographer made them feel important.*

High, But Not on Life – *As I finished taking a picture of someone else, I turned around and saw this young man standing behind me. He was very disoriented and had trouble walking, but I could smell no alcohol on his breath. You would think a person in this condition would shy away from cameras, but he frequently followed me around.*

Smiling Man – *In the mid-1970s, Uptown was truly a racial melting pot. Many other Chicago neighborhoods were dominated by a single ethnic group; Uptown had more diversity than the United Nations. This quiet Hispanic man seemed to be a gentle soul. He spoke little or no English and signed my model release form with an X.*

Social Climbers – *These sociable young men climbed up to the roof of a garage or shed behind their apartment building. When I walked past, they startled me. I wasn't expecting anyone to be sitting up there. They seemed quite proud of their accomplishment. Later they climbed the tree to the left. I think there's a brief period in the life of all kids, male and female alike, when they like to climb trees. The novel perspective helps them see the world from different angles. The climb gives them a sense of accomplishment.*

Guatemalan Restaurant – *This lady ran a restaurant on Wilson Avenue with the help of her daughter. I stopped in on a cold day to change rolls of film. The mother who barely spoke English invited me to take some pictures of her and her daughter preparing food in the warmth of their kitchen. The restaurant was not busy at the time, so they insisted I sit down and have some empanadas with them. During the four years that I photographed in Uptown, I constantly marveled at how generous the people were who had so little to give.*

Dressed for Church – *I found these two dressed in their finest clothes, going to church one Sunday morning with their father (out of frame). The image was taken on North Broadway in January, 1975, as it was starting to snow.*

Lost in Shadows – *One day after dropping off some prints upstairs in this apartment building, I found this young man at street level. I remember thinking that he seemed lost in the harsh, deep shadows. For me, he symbolized the life of kids growing up in Uptown. The "L/K" on the wall was placed there by Latin Kings to signify that this was their turf. This contributed to the fear I saw in this young boy's eyes.*

Relaxing at Wilson and Broadway – *This is the man on the cover. Shortly after I photographed him praying, he sat and spread his legs. He was suddenly emotionally exhausted. Notice how the pedestrians on the street in the background walk far away from the buildings. During this era in Uptown, this was a precaution that many people took to avoid unpleasant surprises from people who might be lurking in doorways.*

Pages 80-81

Young Man by Car – *Cars and driving are a right of passage for young people. In Uptown, poverty delayed that right of passage for many. Here, a man leans against his car, showing it off. I was struck by how immobile his face was. He stood rigidly and his face didn't move from one frame to the next.*

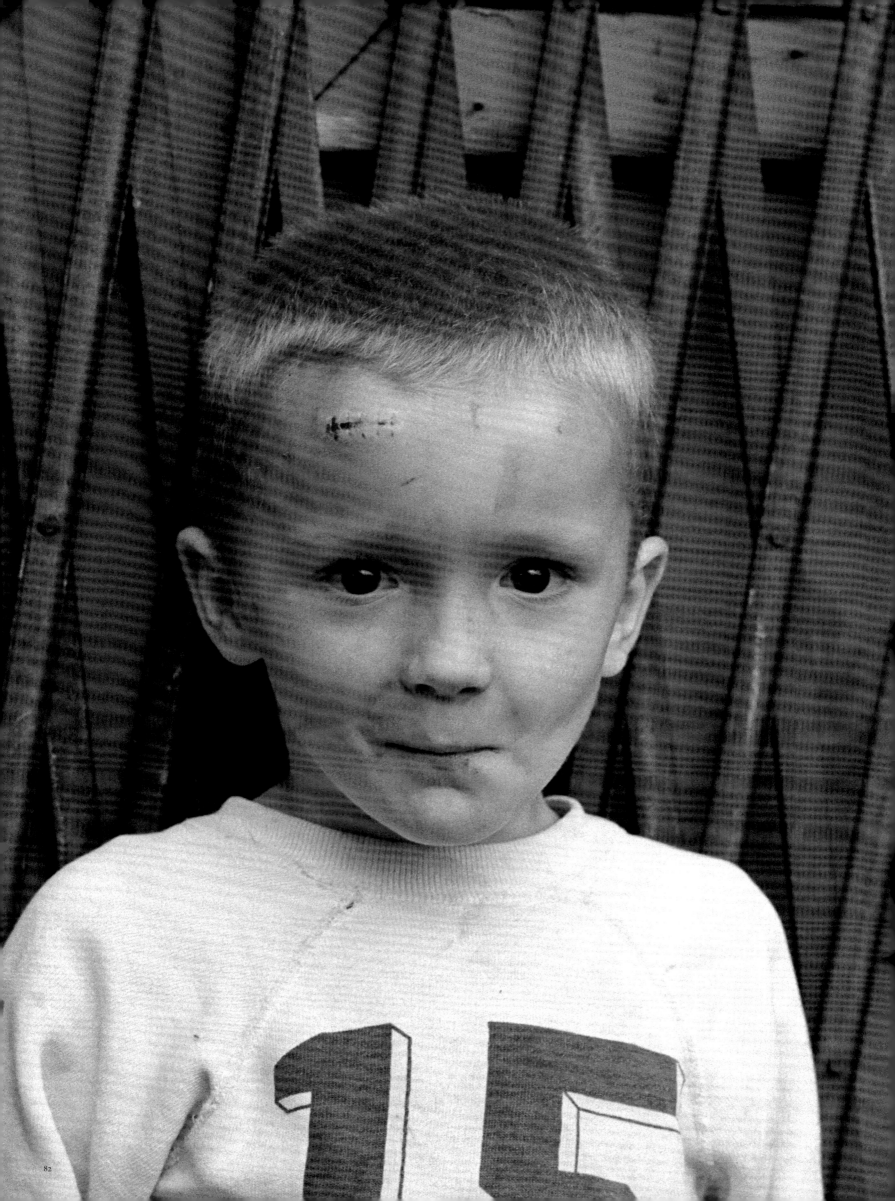

The Exterminators – *Exterminators did a booming business in Uptown during the middle part of the 1970s. The aging housing stock and garbage strewn on the streets attracted insects and vermin. Exterminators had more job security than most in those days.*

Scarred for Life? – *I'm sure the physical scar on this young boy quickly healed. One can only wonder whether the emotional scars from the attack healed as quickly. He told me that someone hit him, but would not tell me who.*

Strong, Silent Type – *This teen had ice-water eyes and barely spoke a word to me. Therefore, I have no idea whether it captured the real "him." I usually engaged my subjects in conversation for several minutes before asking permission to photograph them. This helped me understand what image the subject wanted to convey. It also kept me from being attacked by people who might otherwise have resented an intrusion into their lives.*

On Edge – *This man was muttering to himself in front of a halfway house at Wilson and Hazel. He didn't seem violent, but he did seem agitated for reasons that were not clear. One moment, he would close his eyes and rock. The next, he would rant. He was on an emotional roller coaster ride for reasons only he knew. The photo was taken in 1975.*

We Serve A FULL OUNCE OF WHISKEY

Pontiac and Port Wine – *Early on a sunny Sunday morning, shortly after getting off the 'L' to start my Uptown sojourn, I spotted these bottles clustered around a lamp post. They were on Broadway across from Goldblatt's Department Store, outside one of the neighborhood's many bars. Port wine is strong and sweet, typically drunk as a dessert wine. The person that drank it evidently had to clear his palette with several beers.*

We Serve A Full Ounce of Whiskey – *This sign caught my eye every time I walked past it. The bartender knew how to market his tavern to an untrusting audience. The sentiments resonated with Uptown's many alcoholics; people were constantly taking advantage of them. Many could not read, but the idea got around nonetheless; it was a popular bar.*

Shorts with Long Socks – *The buckling of the street caught this man's attention long enough for me to grab this shot. Uptown had a "second-hand" economy in this era. Many residents could barely afford food. Most of the poor shopped for clothes in the neighborhood's numerous resale shops and rummage stores. Fashion coordination was not their highest priority.*

Knife Game – *This was one of three kids I found playing a knife game; they called it "Domino Peg." Each would take turns balancing the knife on a different part of his body, such as a finger, knee or shoulder. They would then flip the knife so that (hopefully) it stuck in the dirt. The game required each player to estimate the speed of rotation to successfully peg the knife in the ground. Photo taken near Leland and Kenmore on September 7, 1975.*

Young and Old – *As I was photographing the older woman ranting about Chicago politics, the young lady in the halter top walked through my frame. The older lady stopped ranting long enough to smile at the younger one and perhaps remember happier days in her own youth. Uptown in the 1970s was full of ironies like these.*

Jail-O – *This young woman had just gotten off the 'L' at Wilson and was enjoying her cigarette while window shopping. Her T-shirt caught my eye. It must have had some significance for her. Tension between police and Uptown residents was high in this era, but I wasn't sure if the T-shirt was mocking "the system" or the brand.*

Punch Out – *This lady had just been punched in the mouth by her husband and knocked to the ground right in front of me. He grabbed money from her purse and then ran into a bar (behind me) for a shot of whiskey. After I helped the woman to her feet, she asked me if I would give her some money to buy food for her child. I gave her a dollar for letting me photograph them. She literally ran into the bar to join her husband for a drink and left the child on the street.*

Muscle Man – *I encountered this pair going into their apartment building. As soon as they saw my camera, they both struck poses. She smiled. He pretended to be Mr. America. Kids, because they are powerless in a world ruled by grown ups, all want to be bigger than they really are. This is especially true in poor neighborhoods.*

Lawrence and Broadway – *My main objective in Uptown was to capture the spirit of the neighborhood by photographing the people who comprised it. So I didn't take many pictures of streets, but this was one of them. It was a very cold day and people didn't want to linger on the street. Note the Goldblatt's Department Store beyond the Uptown National Bank. The Riviera theater was playing "Snow White." Christmas decorations adorn the light poles.*

Street Ballet – *This woman had just come from a dance class across the street. When I asked if I could take her picture, she struck this playful pose like the prima ballerina in a street ballet. The photo was taken at Sheridan and Broadway in December, 1975.*

Burned Out – *In January of 1975, I found this burned out apartment building at 4136 North Broadway. It was starting to snow and very cold. I pitied the poor families who lost their homes. Note how the plywood that was sealing off the building had been removed. Abandoned buildings became favorite places for drug dealing.*

Slumlord Protest – *On February 28, 1976, the South Andersonville Improvement Association organized a protest against slumlords outside Truman College. WGN-TV covered it. At the rally, numerous residents passed out literature alleging horrific living conditions in the area's tenements. Problems included leaky plumbing, holes in walls, rats, not enough heat, no hot water, bad odors, burned out mattresses, garbage littering property, and more. Protesters also alleged that they were charged exorbitant rents to live in these squalid conditions. The objective of the rally was to get the City to enforce building code violations. See the related story on the following page.*

Bombed? – *I shot this on the southwest corner of Wilson and Magnolia on April 22, 1976. People in the neighborhood alleged the building was "bombed." I was never able to confirm this.*

However, arson in Chicago increased 182% between 1974 and 1977. The increase was so alarming that the state senate adopted a resolution on December 12, 1976, directing the Illinois Legislative Investigating Commission to explore causes and make recommendations.

The Commission's final report in May, 1978, begins with, "The news media has made the public painfully aware of the impact of arson in Chicago's ... Lakeview and Uptown neighborhoods. Charred shells of buildings line blocks of these communities – the sad remains of arson-for-profit schemes, indiscriminate vandalism and revenge fires."

The 145-page report cites numerous reasons for the increase:
- *Recession*
- *Poor training of arson investigators*
- *Poor enforcement of housing codes*
- *Inadequate penalties for arsonists*
- *A severe backlog of cases in housing court*
- *Vandalism of abandoned properties*
- *Cursory investigations*
- *Poorly staffed crime labs*
- *Legal penalties that forced insurance companies not to delay payments in cases of suspected arson*
- *Legislative loopholes that allowed slumlords to operate for years without maintaining their properties or paying taxes.*

After the Commission submitted its final report in 1978, the Legislature remedied many of these issues.

The report also noted several incidents of terrorism. Between June 1975 and May 1978, it says that Chicago had at least 17 terrorist acts of arson by explosives, allegedly committed by a Puerto Rican liberation movement known as Fuerzas Armadas de Liberacion National (FALN), which translates as the "Armed Forces of National Liberation."

House Report 106-488 from the U.S. Government Printing Office indicates that the FALN had a safehouse and bomb-making factory at 736 West Buena in Uptown.

I have no evidence that the incident shown here was related to the FALN or was even a bombing. I mention the FALN because it was a part of the milieu that affected the lives of Uptown residents during this period.

Urban Renewal – *In the 1970s, the focus of urban renewal in Chicago was farther south than Uptown. Young professionals were buying up brownstones on the Near North Side, renovating them and selling them for a tidy profit. As the tidal wave of renovation, fueled by cheap, run-down properties, swept north, it was inevitable that Uptown would stage a comeback. By the late 1970s, a few urban pioneers began redeveloping properties here. This arch sticking out of the rubble of a recently torn down building symbolized both the proud past and promising future of Uptown.*

Four Friends – *America struggled with segregation, integration and racial violence in the 1970s. However, during the entire four years I photographed in Uptown, I can't recall hearing one racial epithet. People would certainly refer to others by their race or nationality, but never in a derogatory fashion. Perhaps this was because they had experienced so much discrimination themselves. Even the Latin Kings and Latin Eagles were racially integrated. I found these four friends chatting in front of an apartment building. After I snapped this shot, the two women went inside and the men went off in another direction. The location was around 920 West Leland. The building in the foreground has been replaced and the building under construction in the middle is Uplift High School.*

North Shore Railroad Tracks – *I took this photo in 1975 on opening day for the Cubs near Wrigley field. These are North Shore Railroad tracks at Byron and Seminary that were abandoned in 1963. The tracks survived into the early 1990s. Portions of the bridge over Montrose still survive to this day. But the area you see here is now a linear park.*

Pages 104-105
Alta Vista – *This block was designated as a historic district in 1971. Unlike the neighborhoods around it, this street has changed little since World War II. Every townhouse on one side of the street is duplicated with only minor variations on the diagonally opposite end. This distinctly human scale creates a tranquility rarely found elsewhere in Chicago.*

Pages 106-107
Progress? – *By the mid-1970s, a few older Uptown apartment buildings were being torn down to make way for newer ones. Developers and real estate brokers expected that the wave of redevelopment sweeping Near North neighborhoods would soon extend to Uptown. They were snapping up bargain basement properties with the expectation that they could soon flip them for a large profit.*

Grace Near Seminary – *I stumbled across this high-walled enclosure on Grace near Seminary while exploring the neighborhood after a Cubs game. It had a peaceful, serene feeling amidst all the chaos of Uptown. A person who lived across the street told me that behind these walls, Roman Catholic nuns ran a home for unwed mothers.*

Urban Hikers – *I found these three kids on Sheridan Road just north of Leland on April 13, 1975. They told me they were "hiking the City." Kids were taught to walk together for protection in those days. They looked like they had enough gear in the backpacks to make it to Montana.*

Painter – *In the summer of 1975, this painter had just finished a hard day's work. I found him outside Kenmore Liquors at 1040 West Wilson, near the corner of Kenmore and Wilson. There was also a bar attached to the liquor store called the Tap Room.*

Latin Kings with Little Kid – *I found these Latin Kings with a young boy on the corner of Winthrop and Ainslie in 1976. Gangs were an ever-present factor in the lives of kids growing up in Uptown. Gang members were often the dominant role models in the lives of kids. The man on the left described himself as a leader of the Latin Kings in this neighborhood. Note that he is wearing a softball shirt that says, "Unknowns." This may have been the precursor for an offshoot (no pun intended) of the Latin Kings called the Insane Unknowns.*

Kids Playing in Alley – *These two kids were playing in the alley behind their family's restaurant, the Guatemala Cafe at 1027 West Wilson. It was a family operation run by their grandmother, mother and father. This family was one of the most welcoming that I met during my four years of photographing in Uptown. Even though their restaurant was modest, their hospitality was outstanding.*

Big Hug – *In May, 1975, at Magnolia and Wilson, this woman had two different men chasing after her. The man who is hugging her had just fended off another as I walked up. The winner gave her a big hug which may have amounted to unwanted affection.*

Proud of His Fingernails – *I encountered this shy man on the street. He hardly spoke at all, but seemed quite pleased that I was paying attention to him. When I asked to take his picture, he stuck out his hands. He was quite proud of his fingernails and the fresh coat of polish.*

Brother and Sister – *I found these two on Wilson Avenue just east of Clark Street. As soon as I photographed them, they scampered back into the beauty shop behind them. Clark was a psychological dividing line between neighborhoods in those days. Parents who lived west of Clark would not let their kids play east of Clark because the streets seemed so much rougher.*

Japanese Man Leading Daughter – *On Argyle near the "L" in 1975, I found a Japanese man leading his daughter by letting her hold his cane. She was hanging on tight. Despite the presence of her father, I got the impression that the neighborhood scared her.*

Apartment Hotel Resident – *In February, 1976, I photographed this lady outside an apartment hotel at 831 West Wilson. Despite cold and her crutches, she was desperate to get some fresh air. Note the five digit phone number with the two letter prefix.*

Lobby of Apartment Hotel – *831 West Wilson had obviously seen better days. The manager hid behind a plywood and metal cage and they no longer accepted cash. Ironically, hotels like this made Uptown an attractive place to live for young professionals in the 1920s. As Uptown aged, the hotels began catering to the City's less fortunate. The small apartments were all they could afford.*

Shopping Friends – *On February 14, 1976, I took this shot of two old ladies. The location was near Sheridan and Irving Park. The neighborhood has changed so much today, it's hard to find this spot.*

Litter Kings – *Chicago's Uptown neighborhood was filled with Latin Kings in the mid-1970s. The neighborhood was also filled with Litter Kings. This stairwell was filled waist high with litter. Such litter existed everywhere in Uptown during this era. Its constant visibility helped to depress property values.*

Bearded Man – *This man's beard made him look like a cross between an Irish elf and Santa's helper. His eyebrows were almost as long as his beard! I photographed him near Sheridan and Broadway in the winter of 1976.*

Hunchback Lady – *I found this lady bowed by life and time, scurrying home with her groceries. I scared her when I tried to talk to her, but she permitted me to take this shot even though she never slowed down. Only after developing the film did I notice all the handwritten signs in the shop window.*

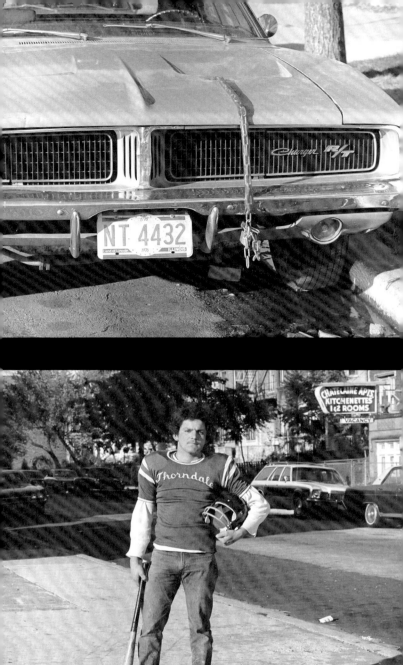
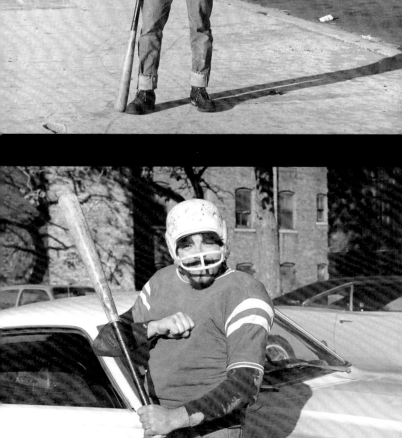

Revenge of the TJOs – *The Thorndale Jagoffs (TJOs) were an Edgewater gang in the 1970s. The Latin Kings around Winthrop and Ainslie in Uptown were their enemies. The Kings stole the battery from this TJO car so often that the TJOs chained the hood down. Then they donned their battle gear and came to Uptown for a fight. Finding no Latin Kings, they decided to urinate on the Kings' mural instead.*

Chippewa – *This man hung out at the corner of Kenmore and Wilson. He had no permanent home and listed his address on my model release form as "In care of Indian Employment Service at 1024 W. Wilson, Suite 212, Chicago, Ill. 60640."*

Babushka – *I found this lady returning to her apartment from a shopping trip on Wilson west of the 'L' near the fire station. When I asked her if I could take her picture, she proudly posed like a fashion model as if she were on a Paris runway, modeling a new coat she had just bought at Goodwill and her babushka. After developing the film, the negative was so hard to look at that I threw it in some bleach. As I watched the image start to dissolve, I had second thoughts. I put it back in some fixer. The bleach, however, had partially reduced the silver halides in the negative, giving this image an ethereal, almost dreamlike quality.*

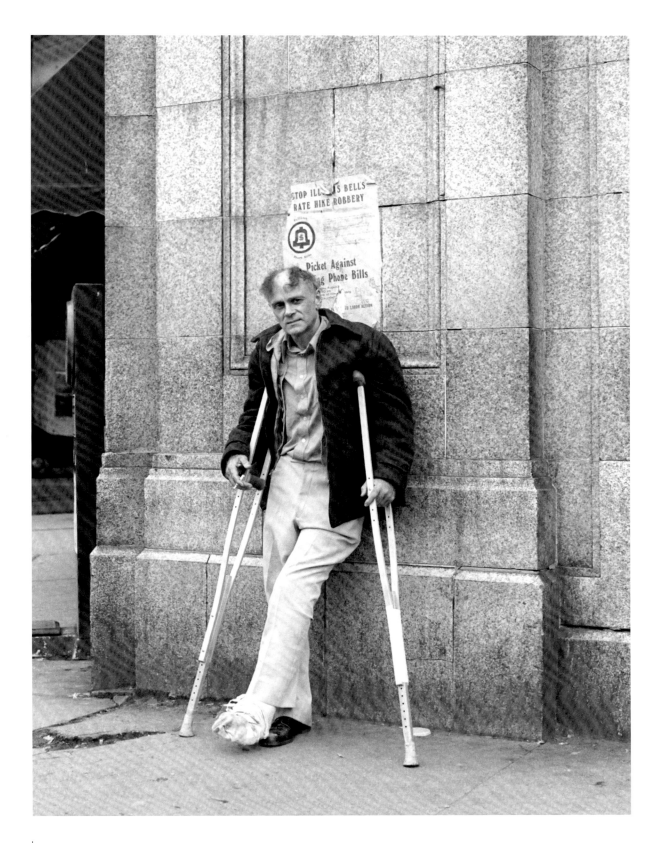

Losing It – I found this poor man near the Wilson 'L' stop on December 14, 1974. He was barely coherent. He had lost everything in his life, including his job, his wife and his hair. He was heartbroken and "losing it." You can read the agony in his expression. I paid him a dollar for signing my model release form, urged him to get some help, and never saw him again.

Gypsy and Baby – *This lady invited me into her apartment to photograph her with her son. It was one of the more bizarre photos in a bizarre series … for obvious reasons. Note the bowling statue next to the gargoyle, religious icons and baby bottle on the mantle above a fireplace which held a wood burning stove. It's hard to imagine anything clashing more than the mother's dress, wallpaper and curtains.*

Hungarian Matriarch – *Uptown was populated largely by Native Americans, African-Americans, poor Southern Whites from Appalachia, and Hispanics. However, many people from eastern Europe had also migrated here. I met and photographed many Hungarians, including this lady who lived in a small apartment with a large, extended family. I felt a lot of love in this home despite the overcrowding. When you look at this woman's smile, you can see where it came from.*

The Original Bargain Basement – *On one of my first days of photographing in Uptown during the mid-1970s, I found a resale shop specializing in clothing for 25 cents. Uptown in that era had an abundance of bars, resale shops, pawn shops and currency exchanges that catered to those in need. Nothing went to waste.*

No Parking, Street Cleaning – *Life in Uptown during the mid-1970s was filled with little ironies. I found this disheveled man sitting on a curb directly under a sign that said, "No Parking, Street Cleaning." He was lighting up what appeared to be the world's longest cigarette. He wasn't wearing socks. This was a style favored by many cost-conscious Uptown residents.*

Bar Brawler – *I saw this man with his friend stumble out of a bar on Wilson Avenue on April 26, 1975. The smaller man was helping the larger who was bleeding profusely. He had obviously been in a bar brawl. He claimed that he gave more than he got. If he won, I would hate to see the guy who lost.*

Assinoboine – *This Native American from the Assinoboine tribe in northern Montana had stoic features that looked as though they were chiseled out of stone. He missed Montana, but needed the work in Chicago. Uptown during the 1970s had a large Native American population, but it has largely dispersed throughout Chicago now.*

Pages 134-135
Cubs Vs. Astros, August 23, 1975 – *This is how baseball should be played – outdoors in the fresh air. On this warm summer day, the Cubs played the Astros. They lost 14 - 12, but it was a nail-biter. The Cubs scored six runs in each of the seventh and eighth innings. No one left early.*

Weary Bones – *This elderly woman had just returned from a shopping trip downtown and needed a rest. I shot this image in 1974, 16 years before the Americans with Disabilities Act (ADA). The Wilson 'L' station of that era was designed to move large numbers of people quickly; few accommodations were made for the elderly or the disabled.*

The Laundromat – *Washers and driers were a luxury that few Uptown residents or apartment buildings could afford in the 1970s. People usually washed their clothes in laundromats like this one near Wilson and Kenmore. This man frequently hung out here. It was warm and he had a captive audience to talk to.*

Arnie Yusim Chevrolet on Broadway – *I bought my first new car from the man on the right while photographing on Broadway. A Chevette caught my eye. It was Chevy's first compact hatchback design – a response to small Japanese vehicles sweeping America after the OPEC oil embargo in 1973. Commercials for the vehicle featured a tall woman and man saying, "I'm 6'4" and my husband is 6'6", yet we both fit in this Chevette." My emotional response was, "No way," so I stopped to look at it. The salesman on the right convinced me to try it. Not only did I fit in the vehicle, at one point, I even managed to put a 108" stainless steel darkroom sink into it. The American car industry was much maligned at the time, but I loved that car and it served me well for many years.*

New Shoes – *Despite the crumbling concrete all around him, this man seemed quite happy as he showed off his new (second hand) shoes to all of his neighborhood friends near Wilson and Hazel.*

Sleeping Girl – *This is perhaps the most uncomfortable sleeping position I have ever seen. But hey, a girl needs her beauty sleep!*

King of Beers – *Uptown had more bars per block in the 1970s than any neighborhood I have ever seen before or since. This poor man was a regular in an establishment at Argyle and Kenmore that proudly advertised Budweiser, the King of Beers. He was on the ragged edge of life. He could barely talk and made a wailing sound like a siren.*

Pages 142-143
Pawn Shop Reclaimed – *The Uptown Pawn Shop at 1022 West Wilson had just moved to greener pastures a couple miles north to the area just south of Loyola. It didn't take vandals long. With the burglar bars removed, the shop was quickly looted and destroyed. The bar next door is also gone. Note how an old coat was stuffed over the air conditioner as insulation.*

OF VALUE
1020 WILSON Inc.
AIR CONDITIONED
Schlitz ON TAP
Confidential
LOANS
1022
ONLY 2 MILES NORTH ON BROADWAY
LARGER NEWER & BETTER
COME ON IN and SEE!
MOVED TO 6350 NORTH BROADWAY
COME ON OVER LET US HELP YOU!
CAMERAS
RADIOS
STEREOS
Televisions

Ambulance at Wilson Club Hotel for Men – *This man's face looked as white as linens, but at least a sheet wasn't over his head. In the mid-1970s, ambulances were common at the hotel which served men who were "down on their luck." It advertised rooms for 75 cents per night. I wasn't allowed inside with my camera, but many people told me living conditions there were deplorable and described it as a flophouse.*

Bed and Buddies – *I was photographing two of these kids with their mother in an adjacent room while the other two waited. The family photos were a bust. The kids frowned in every shot; they obviously wanted to play with their friends. The mother and I gave up. The kids then ran into a bedroom and jumped onto this bed in a joyous heap and started tickling each other.*

Gangs Will Be Gangs — *Kids join gangs for many reasons: for friendship, companionship, a sense of belonging, power, money, parties, girls, and more. On these pages you see: (top) two brothers and their sister. The one on the left was a Latin King; the one on the right a Harrison Gent. Both are showing the signs of their respective gangs and both are now dead. The next image (immediately above) shows a mock execution staged for my sake. Both men are Latin Kings, but one was wearing a captured Latin Eagles' sweater. The emblem is sewn on upside down as a sign of disrespect. (Opposite) Two Latin Kings demonstrate their handshake with fingers connecting in the shape of their symbolic crown.*

The Professor – *This Latin King went by the gang name "Professor." I took this photo near Winthrop and Ainslie in 1976. He had just painted the mural behind him which featured some poetry – a little highbrow for street gangs even if "meant" was misspelled. The Latin King gang sweaters and patches were quite well made. They were higher in quality than the letter sweaters at Northwestern.*

Discos Regalos – *I took this shot at Sheridan and Irving Park in February of 1976. Two young boys were window shopping at this record and gift store. At the time, music was still distributed on vinyl records. Compact disks had just been invented, but didn't become a commercially viable medium until 1982 when Sony and Philips unified their competing formats. During this era, Chicago's Near North was being redeveloped and many Hispanics, especially those of Puerto Rican descent, were being pushed north toward Uptown to find more affordable rents. The Young Lords occupied a storefront at Grace and Wilton at the time – about four blocks away.*

General Contractor – *During the mid-1970s, Chicago's redevelopment was sweeping north through the Belmont area. Young urban professionals were starting to look at Uptown as the next hot spot, a place where you could still find bargain properties, fix them up, and flip them for a handsome profit. This general contractor, I'm sure, was trying to capitalize on what he thought was a promising trend. However, the persistent visibility of poverty – and activists fighting to preserve low-income housing for the poor – stymied redevelopment for decades.*

Fixer Upper – *This house near Winthrop and Ainslie was a hangout for neighborhood kids and gangs. By the mid-1970s, Uptown's housing stock was deteriorating badly. The visibility of the poor, the impaired, gangs and garbage discouraged most investors who sought safer harbors for their money.*

Two Old Friends – *One of these men lived on Wilson Avenue, the other on Ainslie. They insisted that I take several shots of them with their dog. After I did so, they put the dog down and hugged each other for reasons I did not understand but which probably had something to do with alcohol. I think they were drinking buddies. Of course, they could have just been feeling the holiday spirit. I shot this just three days after Christmas in 1974.*

Guatemalan Girl – *This shot was taken in the kitchen of the Guatemala Cafe on Wilson. The pensive girl was helping her mother, the restaurant's owner, prepare empanadas. Notice her apron. I was struck by her shyness compared to the bravado shown by so many Uptown boys. Her family was gracious and welcoming. They insisted I eat some empanadas before I left.*

Bruce Lee and David Carradine Imitators – *Chicago's Uptown was a tough neighborhood in the mid-1970s. Many of the young men worshiped Bruce Lee and David Carradine. Lee was a martial arts movie star who died in Hong Kong in 1973, the year I took these shots. Carradine starred in a hugely popular ABC television series called "Kung Fu" that began airing in 1972. Carradine played a Shaolin monk who roamed the American West looking for a lost brother. Although he intended to avoid notice, he wound up fighting for justice and protecting underdogs wherever he found them. Uptown was a neighborhood full of injustice and underdogs.*

Hasidic Man – *At one time, Uptown had been quite elegant. In the 1920s, many of Chicago's elite built mansions there and the area was known as an entertainment district. During the 1950s and 1960s, most of the middle class had moved north to Rogers Park or the suburbs. By the 1970s, the neighborhood had changed significantly. Still some of the older residents remained. This Jewish man proudly wore his faith. The collision of cultures in Uptown never failed to amaze me.*

Scarface – *I photographed this man on my first visit to Uptown. He looked as though he had seen his share of bar brawls. Because of his scar, I thought he would refuse to let me take his picture. However, he was flattered. I found people in Uptown much more open than suburbanites. This man was a construction worker, if I remember correctly.*

At Ease! – *I know little about this man. He allowed me to take several shots of him, but looked like he was standing at attention the whole time. He told me nothing about himself. Many people in Uptown had pasts that they didn't want to divulge for a variety of reasons. I quickly learned not to pry if people didn't feel like talking.*

Martial Artist – *This young man was part of a large Hungarian family that I photographed often. He was always eager to have me photograph him in martial arts poses. I had just finished photographing some other members of his family, when he came out of the bedroom with a bright red scarf tied around his mid-section. He used the wad of paper dangling from the cloth above him to practice his kicks.*

Christmas Eve at the Salvation Army – *On Christmas Eve in 1974, the line to get into the Salvation Army for dinner stretched out the door and down the block. The Salvation Army did wonderful work in Chicago's Uptown neighborhood. Were it not for them, many more people would have gone hungry.*

Gypsy Woman – *This young woman belonged to a gypsy family shown in several other shots. Three generations lived in a small apartment. I counted at least nine family members. They spoke little English. I believe she is the sister of the boy on the right. She had a baby of her own.*

Boy Scout – *Amid Uptown's poverty, people struggled to keep their kids on the right path. This young man came from a large family. His mother invited me to take pictures of the family. When she told the kids to get dressed in their best clothes, this boy put on his scout uniform. He didn't quite get his hair combed, the shirt tucked in, or the collar turned down. His expression shows a universal feeling among boys when their parents force them to dress up for pictures.*

Uptown Girl – *This woman was at Broadway and Wilson on Christmas Eve of 1974, doing some last minute Christmas shopping for her family. She seemed too well dressed for the neighborhood. Billy Joel didn't record the song Uptown Girl until nine years later, but the lyrics could have been about her. They're about a downtown, working-class man trying to woo a high-class woman from Uptown.*

Barney the Baker – *Uptown had few bakeries in the mid-1970s. Barney ran one on Wilson. Late in the day on December 21, 1974, as people were scurrying home, I saw him feeding pigeons leftovers. He specialized in delicious breads, birthday cakes and pastries. Barney always seemed happy, as you might expect for someone who brought so much joy into people's lives.*

Pages 168-169
Black Panther – *Just before Christmas in 1974, I took this photo of a white man collecting money for the Black Panthers. The Black Panther movement started in the Bay Area in 1966, but quickly spread across the country in the early Seventies. The Black Panther newspaper had a circulation of 250,000 at its height and was edited by Eldridge Cleaver. The button on the man's lapel was a political campaign button for Jose Cha Cha Jimanez who was running for alderman after opening an Uptown Community Service Center.*

Couch Riders – *This was taken in 1974, years before the first video games were invented and when most TVs in Uptown would have been black and white. The kids were couch riders, not couch potatoes. I found them in a vacant lot playing on an abandoned couch that had been thrown from the fourth floor of an apartment building. They tried to make the couch balance on its edge as long as they could before it fell forward or backward. This was not easy with so many kids. One would lean forward while the other leaned back. Every time the couch fell to the ground, they erupted in bursts of laughter. One of the people in the photograph who is now a social worker emailed me to say, "We could find fun in anything!"*

Stop Sign – *I have never been certain of the symbolism in this shot. Sometimes I see a gate keeper. Sometimes I see "arrested development." Regardless, it was certainly difficult for young people to flourish in Uptown during this era. Many lacked parents or other role models to keep them on a positive path.*

Pay Phone – *This series of photographs was taken 20 years before cell phones became ubiquitous. During this era, if you wanted to phone home, you used a pay phone. Pay phones were also popular places for young boys to check for forgotten change. Sometimes you would get lucky and find a dime which was enough to buy a candy bar in those days.*

Sleeping on Sidewalk – *The streets of Uptown in the mid-1970s were usually littered – sometimes with paper, sometimes with people. On this summer morning in 1974, I had no sooner gotten off the 'L' at Wilson Avenue when I spotted this man sleeping (or more likely passed out) on the sidewalk in front of a bar. Scenes like this were so common that, as I paused to take a picture, someone walked through the frame without even glancing.*

Living and Sleeping in Car – *On Wilson Avenue near the 'L', I found this man living and sleeping in his car during the summer of 1974. Both the man and the car had seen better days. He is sleeping with a towel for a blanket. This car might have been the only accommodation in Chicago less expensive than the 75 cent per night cubicles in the Wilson Club Hotel for Men (upper right). Notice how he parked strategically – across from Goodwill, two bars, and a day-labor agency. The open door served as air conditioning.*

Tipping the Scales – *Despite the violence and poverty in Uptown, there were many normal people. I could tell immediately that there was genuine love between this father and his daughter. The presence of such parental love tipped the scales for many kids. Without it, they would not have had a chance. They would have been doomed to drugs, drink and gangs. As the famous basketball coach John Wooden used to say, "Young people need role models, not critics."*

Day Labor — In the mid-1970s, day-labor agencies were a staple of employment for Uptown residents who lived on the economic edge. I talked to one 13-year-old girl who screwed caps on shampoo bottles to help feed her family. The agency paid her $10 for a 12-hour day. No one asked how old she was and she didn't tell.

Deconstruction Worker – *This man worked on the crew tearing down the old Bissets Department Store on the corner of Wilson and Broadway. In late December, it was cold, bone-jarring work. Day-labor agencies sometimes hired people out for demolition work, but specialized in temporary help for manufacturers, shippers, warehousers and remodelers.*

Two More Day-Labor Agencies – *This shot underscores the number of day-labor agencies in Uptown during the mid-1970s. It shows two more next to each other. Employers called such agencies when they needed unskilled help. I recall one year, on opening day at Wrigley Field, when it snowed badly. Day-labor agencies like these supplied workers from Uptown to shovel the stands and sidewalks.*

The Four Amigos – *Young kids constantly roamed the streets of Uptown without adult supervision. This was an era of hyperinflation. It jumped from 6.16% in 1973 to 11.03% in 1974. To help feed families, many woman were forced to work. In better times, they might have stayed home to raise children.*

Dressed Up – *I photographed this young man in 1974 on Winthrop. He was quite fashionably dressed for the standards of the era and neighborhood. Perhaps he was all dressed up to impress a new girlfriend. He was definitely making a fashion statement.*

Knit Beret – *I photographed this young man in the 4800 block of North Winthrop during the summer of 1974. He was with a group of friends – both male and female – who were well dressed in the styles of the time. I suspect one of the women, who may have been his girlfriend, knit the beret. He's wearing a heart-shaped medallion around his neck.*

Afro Haircut — *Afros were very popular in the 1960s and 1970s. Men competed with each other to see how big they could make them grow. There's a practical limit, however, to these high-maintenance haircuts. People had to carry "picks" with long teeth and groom themselves constantly. The slightest wind or touch could destroy the symmetry of the ball. Nevertheless, they were a symbol of emerging African-American pride.*

Pages 184-185
Latin Eagle's Gym — *This group invited me to photograph them in their "clubhouse," a room with a bench press machine and some weights. While the popular image of gangs revolves around violence, gangs also provided a social function. They gave teens a sense of belonging. Here, Uptown's Latin Eagles demonstrate their solidarity by lifting a barbell together, much like soldiers in basic training might lift a telephone pole.*

Peaceful Coexistence — *The term "peaceful coexistence" described the often tense relationship between the Soviet Union and the U.S. during the Cold War. The term could also be applied to Uptown's Latin Kings and Harrison Gents in the mid-1970s. This joint mural on North Winthrop shows a smiling being gently separating the two groups which lived side by side. I saw other examples indicating that the gangs coexisted peacefully: two brothers who were members of the different gangs and a softball team called the Unknowns with members from both gangs. This shot was taken in 1974. The groups later went to war with each other.*

Volunteer – *Some volunteered for the Vietnam War effort out of a sense of patriotism. Others volunteered to learn a job skill, escape the neighborhood, travel, or to get "three hots and a cot." If you didn't have any felonies, it was an easy job to get at a time when the unemployment rate was pushing 8.5%. While I was talking to the recruiter, this aging man tried to join up for the $2,500 bonus.*

Army Recruiter – *In late 1974, during the waning months of the Vietnam War, I photographed this U.S. Army recruiter outside his office at 1056 West Wilson Avenue. The Army could get all the people it needed through the draft lottery that existed at the time. Nevertheless, it maintained an active recruiting campaign to reduce reliance on the unpopular draft. The Army offered $2,500 signing bonuses for high school graduates.*

Sure She Would Win the Lottery – *On July 1, 1974, the new Illinois State Lottery started selling tickets. I photographed this woman on Independence Day that year. She had just bought one of the first lottery tickets and was telling me how the money she was sure to win would transform her life. I hope it did. Next to the lottery sign was another featuring food stamps.*

Wilson Club Hotel for Men – *In 1974, this hotel advertised rooms for 75 cents per night. It attracted people who were "down on their luck" or who were new to the city and looking for work. One alderman claimed it was "not fit for human beings." This young man told me he was living there while he went to vocational school so that he could earn a decent living. It was the only place he could afford.*

Two Men in Pickup — *After photographing the kids at the left, I turned and saw these two men staring at me from their pickup. They gave me an icy, chilling stare. I walked away thinking about the collision of lifestyles and cultures in this neighborhood.*

Roller Derby — *This group of kids turned the corner onto Lawrence Avenue from Broadway about a block in front of me. Half of them had on new roller skates. They were exited beyond belief, feeding off of each other's energy. It's hard to have this much fun on the Internet.*

Smiling Girl – *Uptown's young and old people exuded different feelings. The young were usually happier, more optimistic, more open and more energetic. This beautiful young girl certainly fit that mold. If she hadn't been in Uptown, she could have been in the pages of Vogue.*

Derby Man – *This man made a fashion statement. When I took this photo in 1974, hats like this were very unusual. Plaid pants, however, were in vogue, as were floral shirts and black jackets with wide collars.*

The Huddle – *Few places in Uptown during the mid-1970s had a patch of grass big enough to play football on. I found these four kids playing a game of two-on-two in front of an Uptown church. They took time out to have their picture taken and posed in a huddle. Despite having Lincoln Park nearby, most kids this age played close to home. Many feared walking through streets controlled by unfamiliar gangs.*

Barefoot Mother and Son – *These two were proud to pose for a picture despite the boy's large bandage and missing teeth. Prophetically, his T-shirt features a Peanuts cartoon that says, "I can't even win enough games to have a slump." The number of men in the background leads me to believe they lived in a boarding house. I do not know how his injuries were caused.*

Can We Go Out and Play? – *Many parents who lived in Uptown during the mid-1970s were reluctant to let their kids play on the streets because of real and perceived dangers. It was common to see kids staring out of windows like this, yearning to go out and play.*

Latin Eagle and Girlfriend – *This young man seemed like one of the quieter members of his gang. He never put on a tough face for photos and seemed much more impressed with this young lady than the gang scene. Young women often had a civilizing influence on the young men of Uptown in the 1970s.*

Buena Grocery – *Tucked under the 'L' on the north side of Buena Circle Park, this store advertised Spanish and American foods. However, most of their sales seemed to be snacks. Neighborhood kids hung out here. They usually left their dogs at the door.*

Buena Girl – *This young woman frequently joined the crowd of kids that hung out at the Buena Grocery store near the 'L'. In August of 1974, she was enjoying the last days of summer vacation. I photographed her with a half-dozen other kids who were razzing her good-naturedly while she posed.*

Girl Teasing Boy – *I photographed these two at the same time as the girl above. This girl was a year or two older than the boy and a head taller. As I put the camera up to my eye, she bent her knees so that he would appear taller. However, she left her arm around his shoulders. The awkwardness of it all made them both laugh. I smile every time I see this picture. It's one of my favorites from my four years in Uptown.*

Quizzical – *I found this young man standing by the folding security gate in front of a pawn shop. He seemed very quizzical. He asked me questions about my camera and what I was doing. I was constantly amazed at the number of young children roaming Uptown's streets. They seemed filled with danger, but most of the kids seemed to survive. As Nietzsche said, "What doesn't kill you makes you stronger."*

Father and Daughter – *This young girl and her father were going shopping when I spotted them on Buena near Kenmore. Like many families in Chicago's Uptown neighborhood, they didn't have much, but they had a lot of pride. Their vehicle, though old, was clean and lovingly maintained.*

Wake Up Call – *Drunks often slept in Uptown doorways during the 1970s. Periodically the police would make sweeps of the neighborhood. According to some people I interviewed, the police would take them to the South Side, forcing them to walk home. Scenes like this were a wake-up call for activists trying to maintain their neighborhood and property values which were also heading south.*

Peekaboo – *This young woman seemed genuinely happy. She stared straight at me through a shock of hair and made no attempt to remove it, confident that I would capture her inner strength despite the obstacle.*

Recycling, Uptown Style — *Scenes like this were common in Uptown during the mid-1970s. People wasted nothing. They stripped dead vehicles to keep other vehicles rolling. Recycling was done out of economic necessity, not to help the environment.*

Oasis of Solace — *Amid all the poverty, strife and craziness that was Uptown in the 1970s, I came across this old Japanese man tending his garden. A Japanese-American friend of mine called it an oasis of solace.*

Salute of Stars – *I shot this in 1974 in an alley off Wilson Avenue. The man didn't mind being called a drunk but hated the term wino. He had spent six years in the service and told me, "It's easier to live behind the gun than not." This was a reference to the regimentation of military life which he missed. He was proud of the fact that he had never been on welfare, but said it was hard to find day-labor jobs in the summer because the kids took them all. Sitting and sipping in the alley between Mayor Daley's Salute of Stars and a pawn shop sign symbolized the plight of Uptown's less fortunate.*

Uptown Broadway Building – *On the east side of Broadway, just north of Leland stands one of the most magnificent buildings in Uptown, a remnant from the neighborhood's Gilded Age. It was built in 1926. I photographed it in 1976, on its fiftieth anniversary. The building still stands almost 40 years later and is now on the national register of historic landmarks. Its ornate terra-cotta facade depicts ancient gods, rams' heads, shields, helmets, birds, fruits, and trophies. Note the seven-digit phone number on the bank that began with UP.*

Native American – *This American Indian woman had the beautiful, knowing smile of someone who has seen a lot in life. During the 1970s, Uptown was the hub of American Indian life in Chicago. According to the Chicago Tribune, Uptown had more than 20 Indian organizations at the time. Many Native Americans told me that virtually every tribe in America was represented here. Many Indians did not want to have their photographs taken, but this lady didn't mind. They often told me they believed the camera would "capture their spirit." Some years later, I read a passage by Edward Curtis, the great photographer of the American West, who said he frequently encountered this belief, too.*

22 Years without Missing One Home Game – *This amputee told me that he had been passing the hat at this same spot near Wrigley Field for 22 years and that he had not missed one home game during that entire period.*

XXX Rated – *In 1975, adult movie theaters like the Festival near Sheridan and Irving Park in Uptown were a prominent feature of the urban landscape. They largely disappeared with the advent of the Internet.*

Hat Man – *This man ran a dry cleaning and hat cleaning service in Uptown during the mid-1970s. The device in the background was used for pressing hats after they were cleaned. The crown of the hat fit into the metal semi-circle as the press was lowered on the brim. This photo was taken near the end of the era of hats. Shortly after this, they fell out of fashion.*

Shoe Repairman – *This man did a booming business in Uptown during the mid-1970s. Uptown was a very blue collar, working class neighborhood during that era. People would re-sole shoes several times before the uppers gave out.*

Hey Sailor! — *While getting off the 'L' one day, I noticed this sailor staring at a poster for a porn film called "Super Vixen." Perhaps he was heading to Great Lakes Naval Training Station about 40 miles north and a world away.*

Currency Exchange in Wilson 'L' – *Currency exchanges were frequently located near public transportation throughout Chicago during the 1970s. They had little to do with exchanging foreign currency for U.S. dollars. They gave people without bank accounts a way to cash checks and pay bills. They also provided numerous other services for the convenience of customers.*

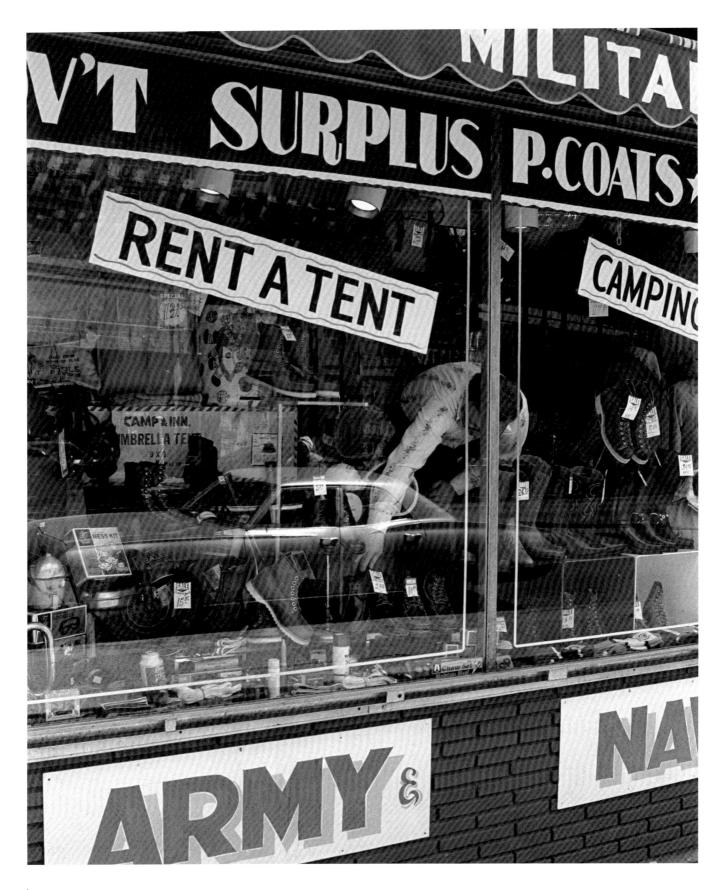

Rent a Tent – *The Z-Wallis Surplus store on Broadway near Leland has survived for decades by knowing its audience. One resident told me she bought brass knuckles here. But I've often wondered if this "Rent a Tent" promotion succeeded. It was not safe to pitch a tent in Uptown. Those who slept in public places risked attack. Of course, they could have been targeting people who wanted to escape the city for a weekend. But getaways in Uptown during this era were usually to the corner tavern.*

Wrong Place, Wrong Time – *This man was in the wrong place at the wrong time. Uptown had many people with alcohol problems in the 1970s. This man told me that he stumbled out of a bar the week before I took this picture and fell asleep on a park bench. He said some teenagers hit him over his head with a beer bottle while he slept, then tried to light him on fire. He felt lucky to survive the burns and the beating.*

Long Line at Aragon – *The day was December 27, 1975. The Blue Oyster Cult and Ted Nugent were playing at the Aragon that night. Teenagers began lining up 24 hours in advance to get good seats. The freezing weather did not diminish their enthusiasm.*

Petered Meter – *Witness one person's rage against The Man. Is there a Chicagoan who doesn't sympathize with this image of a parking meter ripped out of the sidewalk by its roots? Such vandalism was fairly common in Uptown during the mid-1970s.*

"Puerto Ricans are The Best!" – *When I asked these boys to tell me about themselves, the one in the trapeze T-shirt proudly proclaimed that he was Puerto Rican, then added, "Puerto Ricans are the best!" At that point, his friend on the left smiled and their little buddy grimaced as if thinking, "Here he goes again!" I quickly snapped the shot. Uptown in the mid-1970s had a large Puerto Rican population pushed north by the redevelopment of neighborhoods farther south.*

Ready to Party – *This couple had just left one of the many liquor stores on Wilson Avenue. It was early spring in 1975 and everyone was wearing heavy coats except the man carrying the wine. Perhaps he had gotten a head start on the festivities.*

Gyros and Gamma Rays – *Technically, Lincoln Square isn't in Uptown. But one day I got off the 'L' at Lawrence and just walked west for a change. I found this Greek restaurant that doubled as a fallout shelter. Note the radiation sign under the second S. If you grew up during the Cold War, you will remember fallout shelters. They were designed as part of America's civil defense system to protect against nuclear attack. Ouzo probably would have worked just as well and would have cost a lot less.*

The Sensuous Woman – I took this shot in 1974. The girl wearing the T-shirt probably bought it at one of Uptown's many resale shops, thinking it was clever, without fully understanding what it referred to. "The Sensuous Woman" was a best-selling book published in 1969 under a pseudonym about the author's "pursuit of the ultimate in sexual pleasure." It was also the name of Don Gibson's #1 country hit in 1972.

Happiness Is... – ...shade on a hot summer day and a parking meter to lean against. When you don't have a lot, you learn to take joy in life's simple pleasures. Life in Uptown was like free theater. If you stood in one place long enough, something strange would happen. Ironically, this was taken on Broadway, in front of the Uptown Theater.

Bissets Before the Wrecking Ball – *On October 22, 1975, I photographed Wilson from the 'L' at sunrise. It shows Bissets Department Store on the right. Fans of this proud, old store lovingly described the service, high-quality merchandise, and pneumatic tubes that carried money from one area to another.*

Bye-Bye Bissets – *It must have been a sad day for the Bisset family. I took this picture of their building being torn down two months later on December 27, 1975. Many people felt it marked the end of an era, but the store had been closed for several years.*

Pages 234-235
Land Yacht at Wilson 'L' — *Early in the morning of October 22, 1975 this land yacht sailed around the corner of Wilson and Broadway. The OPEC oil embargo in October, 1973, quadrupled oil prices in 1974. Within a year, gas guzzlers like this became the subject of jokes.*

Uptown Observer — *This young man seemed like a keen observer of the world around him. It was as though he was trying to make sense out of so many things that didn't make sense.*

Japanese American — *Uptown was a melting pot. This man lived on West Leland. World War II seems distant now. But in 1976 when I took this picture, there was still a lot of resentment toward Japan because of World War II. The story of Japanese Americans who had been interned during the war – but still volunteered to fight for America – was not widely known. Many joined the 100th Infantry Battalion, the 442nd Regimental Combat team, and the Military Intelligence Service (MIS). These units were among the most decorated in World War II. They played crucial roles in European combat and decoding Japanese communications. But it would take 66 years before Congress recognized their valor with a Gold Medal.*

Love is Blind – *The image of these two teenagers amid Uptown's squalor in the mid-1970s proves that love IS blind. They ignored the trash and graffiti around them. Somehow it didn't matter. They had each other.*

Unhappy – *On December 14, 1974, I photographed this young shopper on Wilson near Sheridan. Christmas must have been difficult for her that year. The OPEC oil embargo in October of 1973 had plunged the nation into a deep recession and high inflation. Inflation soared from 3.65% at the start of 1973 to 12.34% when I took this picture. Holidays like Christmas could be a bittersweet experience for people in Uptown during that era. They brought economic woes into sharp relief.*

Couple at Playground – *I found this young couple watching their friends play basketball at the Stewart School at 4525 Kenmore. He was very proud of her and she of him. Note the bell-bottom jeans which were popular during the late 1960s and early 1970s. The Chicago Board of Education voted to close this school in May, 2013, after lengthy protests by neighborhood residents.*

One Way to Beat a Parking Ticket – *For parking tickets to be enforceable, no parking zones must be clearly marked. If people couldn't find a legal parking spot, they would sometimes rip the no parking sign out of the concrete. I saw this happen more than once in Uptown.*

Greeter – Almost a decade before Walmart popularized the notion of "greeters," this boy greeted me in front of a small grocery store on Wilson Avenue that sold meats, fruits, vegetables, cigars and cigarettes. Note how most of the signs are in Spanish, but the U.S.D.A. food-coupon poster is in English.

Progress – During the mid-1970s, Uptown still had a few of its original residents. I found this man looking wistfully through a construction fence during construction of the Truman College. The site obviously held some emotional significance for him. He may have been recalling happier days spent at the De Luxe Theater on this site. It was built in 1912. Reportedly, Gloria Swanson, the silent movie star, visited the De Luxe frequently when she lived in Uptown. The theater was demolished in 1972.

Behind Door #1 – *To make a living in Uptown in 1975, a professional had to be versatile. This person set the record. While the signs looked crude, they made his services look affordable, which was a key to success during that era.*

Puppy Love – *I photographed hundreds of people with dogs in Uptown. They offered unconditional love, a rare commodity in this area during the mid-1970s. They also offered protection.*

Praying — *This man was pacing back and forth nervously at Broadway and Wilson, muttering to himself. When I asked if I could take his picture, he said, "Sure," dropped to his knees, struck this pose and said, "My name is Jehovah." It all happened so fast that I didn't realize he was missing parts of two fingers until I developed the film.*

Before Video Games – *In the early 1970s when I took this shot, Odyssey had just released the first video game console that could be played in the home on a TV. However, few people in Uptown could afford the games. Kids had only each other to play with.*

Pages 248-249
Run Down – *In 1976, Chris Cohen campaigned for Alderman with the slogan, "A City is For Living." Cohen won the race. He later described the types of calls he took as Alderman. "Some people want more park benches. They want abandoned cars removed; potholes fixed; signs to regulate bicycle, bus and auto traffic; bulk trash removed; and CTA platforms repainted. They have immigration problems, complaints about dogs, about garbage collection. They want new schools, sewers." Today, a parking lot stands on this corner at Wilson and Kenmore.*

Leader of the Pack — *This young man told me he was the head of one of two Latin gangs in Uptown, the Latin Kings. I saw him frequently on the streets with his dogs yet never felt threatened by him or his gang. I gave them free photographs; they gave me free passage.*

Taunt – *Every young boy has had an experience like this. In 1974, I found three kids in an empty Uptown lot. The boy in the middle was teasing the boy on the left. I felt sorry for him and wanted to intervene. However, I realized that the kid in the middle was simply putting on a show for the camera, so I simply grabbed the shot and left. They went back to digging in the dirt.*

945 West Dakin – *In 1976, I took this shot while standing under the 'L'. Technically, this is in Lakeview. However, it served many people in Uptown. It is still an automotive shop today, though its focus has broadened. If 100,000 people take the red line 'L' past this point every day, more than 1.3 billion people have gone by this shop since I took this photo.*

Playing Dead – *I took this shot at the same time as the one to the left. This image of a kid playing dead – but grinning from behind his hand – also felt strangely foreboding to me. Knowing the neighborhood and how the statistics are stacked against African-American teenagers, I feared that it foretold his future.*

Gun Play – *A stroll through Uptown never failed to yield interesting shots. These two were playing with toy guns as virtually all boys do. However, as I took this photo, I felt uneasy. I hoped that this wasn't an omen of things to come for these two.*

Melting Ice Cream Cone – *I remember wondering when I took this shot how vacant this child's expression was. Sadly, it was all too commonplace in Uptown. He didn't even seem all that interested in his ice cream cone which was melting down his hand.*

Shake and Signify – *The two Latin Kings in the background show the gang handshake, which mimics the points of a crown. The one in the foreground is "signifying." Signifying is a sign of recognition. It says, "I belong to the Latin Kings." When strangers met on a street, they would signify as a way of telling friend from foe.*

Young Mother with Two Children — *I found this young loving mother with her two adoring children in a laundromat. She looked like she was barely out of her teens. At first, I thought she might be single. When I developed the film, I noticed the wedding ring on her finger. Even in the Uptown of the 1970s, normal, happy, healthy families managed to survive and thrive despite the obstacles.*

Police Responding to Bar Fight – *I was walking down Wilson just west of the 'L' on September 5, 1974 when a man and a screaming woman spilled out of a bar just in front of me. This shot sums up much of Uptown in the mid-1970s. It shows bars and pawn shops stretching to infinity, currency exchanges, stores accepting food stamps, a bar fight, some people ignoring the fight, others gawking, and police vehicles pulled onto the sidewalk.*

Max Marek – Marek was one of Uptown's most famous residents during the period I photographed there. He went to Notre Dame on a football scholarship and was the only boxer ever to beat Joe Lewis. At one time, Marek was ranked as the #10 heavyweight in the world. He owned an art and curio shop at 3800 North Sheffield on the southern edge of Chicago's Uptown neighborhood. I took this picture in 1976, a year before Marek died. Marek was deeply concerned about the values of people and society, so he started something called the HIHOE Society. HIHOE stood for Heaven Is Here On Earth. While it sounds utopian, a pamphlet he wrote about HIHOE's goals was full of pragmatic advice. For instance, "To keep one man in jail for one year costs $26,000. What a waste of money and lives! We must divert this money into employing people rather than jailing them." Today, the cost per inmate in Illinois is more than $38,000/year; the average per capita annual income is $28,000.

Social Networking Before the Internet – *Few people could afford air conditioning in Uptown. On one hot summer day in 1975, these friends escaped the stifling heat in their apartment building by moving out to the balcony. Balconies were favored places for people-watching. They talked with everyone walking down the street.*

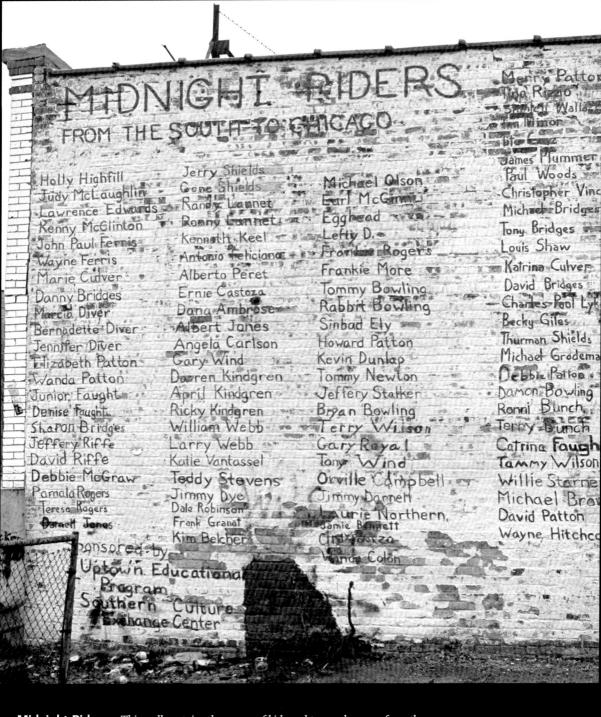

Midnight Riders – *This wall contains the names of kids and teens who came from the South to Uptown. Ever since Paul Revere, political activists, bikers, sports teams, rock bands, messenger services have been calling themselves "Midnight Riders." People moving from the South were called Midnight Riders because they drove during the night to avoid traffic and the heat. Many cars in those days did not have air conditioning. Two of the people on this list recently told me that approximately 20 of these kids died before they were 50.*

Double Amputee – *I'm not sure how this man lost his legs. However, heavy smoking and alcohol use are both risk factors for amputation. As I photographed him, I noted that his fingernails were stained yellow from nicotine and his hands were shaking, probably due to the DTs. He's clasping them to make the shakes less visible. I gave him a dollar for signing my model release and he promptly wheeled himself into a bar to drink it up. A pathologist at Cook County Hospital pointed out a third possible explanation for the high number of amputees in Uptown: frostbite. She saw many alcoholics who passed out in freezing weather who required limb amputation due to severe frostbite.*

Gaylord on Sunnyside – *This young man who went by the street name of "Hound Dog" told me that he belonged to a gang called the Gaylords. In Uptown during the 1970s, Sunnyside was the headquarters for Gaylords. This shot was taken while the Sunnyside Mall was still under construction. Note the broken window in the background. I'm not sure what the package in his hands is. He was gripping it tightly and looking around nervously when I took this shot on April 26, 1975.*

Young Love – *I often saw these two young teenagers on Sunnyside. The young man told me he was a Gaylord who went by the street name of "Drifter." On this day, as I put the camera to my eye, the Drifter immediately slouched into an "I'm cool" posture to impress his girlfriend. She didn't seem to notice or care.*

Out in the Outfield – "Hey, look awake out there." In 1974, I took this shot of three boys playing baseball at the Chicago Pumping Station at Wilson and Marine Drive, south of Weiss Hospital. Someone was passed out in their right field. Undeterred and unphased, they calmly played ball around him. Note how the boys' dog stands vigil between them and the sleeping man.

Latin King Pin – I found this man hanging out on the corner of Withrop and Ainsle with much younger Latin Kings. Despite his age, he proudly wore the insignia of the Kings. Note the diamond pin on his trapeze T-shirt. The jewelry was even more impressive than the fraternity pins worn at Northwestern.

New Hope – *This was one of the last shots I took in Uptown. I photographed this man several times before. He was the Latin King leader. However, on this occasion, he told me he was the ex-leader. I believe he was trying to settle down for the sake of the baby. Each new child has the power to change the world. Some just take longer than others.*

ABOUT THE EQUIPMENT AND TECHNIQUE

Rollei SL66

Equipment

I shot all of these images on film: 80 percent of them with a Nikon F2. Most of those were shot with one of two lenses: the Nikkor 35mm f1.4 or the 105mm f2.5. I used the 105 for shooting close-ups of people and the 35 when I wanted to capture some of the environment. I used other lenses from time to time, but found that the more I carried, the harder it was to shoot. Walking the streets of Uptown for hours at a time quickly turned me into a minimalist when it came to equipment.

The Nikon F2 contained a through-the-lens (TTL) match-needle metering system. A floating needle inside the viewfinder told you how much light was falling on the subject. This was a huge advance in technology at the time. Still, I had to focus and set the exposure manually. When the needle was centered, you had an "average" exposure.

When photographing Caucasians, I typically increased the exposure one stop to make their skin look brighter. For dark skinned people, I reduced the exposure one stop. This kept everyone from looking "middle gray." The center-weighted metering system was designed to take readings from the center of the frame and place them in the middle of the exposure curve, requiring a manual override for correct exposure of skin tones in close-ups.

Although Nikon offered a motor drive for the F2, I could not afford one until 1976. I took the vast majority of these shots manually, one frame at a time. I loved that camera and used it until the late 1990s.

I shot Kodak Tri-X film. While somewhat grainy, it was fast enough (ISO 400) to allow me to shoot handheld in most situations (usually from a 60th to a 250th of a second depending on time of day and cloud cover).

I also used a Rolleiflex SL66. The SL stood for single-lens reflex, meaning you could focus through the lens. The 66 stood for six centimeters by six centimeters, the size of the negative (2¼ inches by 2¼ inches).

Compared to the 35mm Nikon, the Rollei used film that was much bigger. Therefore the prints required less enlargement and the images looked sharper and less grainy at any given size. However, the camera had several drawbacks. It was much heavier, a liability for street photography. It also required the use of a handheld exposure meter, which made photography less spontaneous. Still, shooting with it was a joy because of the large, razor-sharp negatives that made excellent enlargements.

For the ultimate in sharpness, I used a Deardorff 4x5 view camera with Schneider lenses. The Deardorff was manufactured in Chicago and made out of mahogany. The camera itself was a work of art and I still own it.

I took only a handful of shots with the Deardorff because it was so heavy and difficult to set up for street photography. It required carrying a tripod and film holders.

Very few of these shots were taken at night because I could not afford a flash at the time.

Each night I would come home and develop the film in my darkroom. I used Kodak D76 diluted 1:1 with water to reduce the contrast slightly.

For printing, I used Omega enlargers with Schneider lenses.

I made prints using Zone VI Brilliant paper in varying grades of contrast and used selenium toner in the processing to protect them from degradation over time.

Technique

Generally speaking, I would see someone that interested me, then engage the person in conversation and ask permission before taking any photos. The entire process would usually take five or ten minutes. The people of Uptown at the time were open and welcoming, but also suspicious. Trying to sneak shots could have led to ugly confrontations. Brief conversations built a level of trust that encouraged people to open up.

In exchange for signing my model release forms, I would give people a dollar or free prints. I would usually drop off the prints on my next visit to Uptown. On my return, many people would invite me into their homes and businesses to take additional photos.

I paper-clipped release forms plus notes about locations and conversations with subjects to each of my contact sheets. Those notes formed the basis for many of the captions that you read in this book.

Admittedly, walking the streets was the least random form of sampling I could have done. However, by wearing out enough shoes, I collected a series of shots that represent the Uptown of that era.

Deardorff 4x5 view camera with Schneider lenses

ACKNOWLEDGEMENTS

Special Thanks

I would like the thank the people of Uptown for allowing me to photograph them, their neighborhood and their homes. Despite difficult circumstances and times, you were some of the kindest, most welcoming and most open people I have every met anywhere. When I posted many of these images on my photoblog, BobRehak.com, many Uptown residents, both past and current, wrote me to provide details, corrections, and updates about the people and places in the photos. You turned this book into a "collaborative history" making it a much richer experience. There were literally hundreds of you. My heartfelt thanks to you all.

Joanne Asala, editor of the Uptown history blog at CompassRose.org and author of more than 20 books, was among the first to discover this cache of photos. Joanne posted several of my photos on her website and, within days, my website "went viral." This provided the encouragement I needed to undertake this project. She also provided valuable insights into how Uptown had changed in the 33 years since I moved to Texas and introduced me to Chicago's current Alderman from Uptown, the Honorable James Cappleman.

Several other blogs also linked people to my website. Among them: UptownUpdate.com, Calumet412.com and The Living History of Illinois and Chicago.

My thanks also to Neal Samors, my publisher, for his valuable advice and guidance; the many people at Friesens for their printing expertise; Janice Costa for providing valuable psychological insights into the lives of kids growing up in environments like Uptown; Kathy Czubik and Jennifer Gleason for their proofreading; Chris Daigle for his help in retouching and re-sizing film scans; Mike Meyers who always adds beauty and meaning to my words and pictures through his inspired design; and Stephen McFarland for his assistance with research, website development, and help with photographing the cameras that I used in Uptown.

My wife, daughter and son provided valuable input as I developed the text and selected photos. Without their support and understanding, none of this would have been possible.

In a special category, I would also like to thank Tina (Tedesco) Settecase, a college classmate and, later, a Sears executive. Tina and I started a small photography business while still in college. Together, we bought the Rollei SL66 that I used to take many of these photos. Ironically, Tina also introduced me to my wife. One night, while I was developing Uptown photos in my darkroom, Tina brought her over to my apartment. I almost didn't answer the buzzer because I had film in the developer. Thank you, Tina, for being so persistent with that buzzer.